WHAT A LOAD OF TRASH!

BY STEVE SKIDMORE
ILLUSTRATIONS BY THOMPSON YARDLEY

WHAT A LOAD OF TRASH!

THE MILLBROOK PRESS · BROOKFIELD, CONNECTICUT

Cataloging-in-Publication Data
Skidmore, Steve
What a load of trash! rescue your household waste/
by Steve Skidmore; Illustrations by Thompson Yardley.
Brookfield, Conn.: The Millbrook Press, 1991.
40 p.: col. ill;   cm   (A lighter look book)
Includes bibliographical references
Includes index.
Summary: Discusses different kinds of wastes and
their effects on the environment,
as well as ways to dispose of or recycle them.
1. Refuse and refuse disposal—Juvenile literature.
2. Recycling (Wastes, etc.)—Juvenile literature.
3. Incinerators—Juvenile literature.
I. Yardley, Thompson, ill.   II. Title. III. Series.
363.7288
ISBN 1-878841-27-0

First published in the United States in 1991 by
The Millbrook Press Inc.
2 Old New Milford Road
Brookfield, Connecticut 06804
© Copyright Cassell plc 1990
First published in Great Britain in 1990 by Cassell
Publishers Limited as *What a Load of Rubbish!*

WHAT A LOAD OF TRASH!

Like a spaceship, the Earth has only a limited amount of fuel
and supplies. When they have run out, they cannot be replaced.

THEN WHAT WILL WE DO?

Find out what YOU can do about

Saving raw materials!
Protecting the environment!
Waste disposal!
Saving energy!

WHAT HAVE YOU THROWN AWAY TODAY?

WHAT IS TRASH?

Most things you throw away as trash were useful when they were bought.

When you buy cornflakes you have to buy the package as well as the cereal inside!

And then there's that horrible shirt. Somebody else might love it!

The main thing wrong with trash is

MOST PEOPLE
THINK IT'S TRASH!

But clever people know that trash is

VALUABLE! USEFUL!
WORTH SAVING!

So let's dig through some of this stuff we call trash and see who's right!

What would it be like to live in a trash can?
It would be dark and . . .

Some of this is the smell of methane gas!

Methane gas is given off when the
things we throw away start to rot.

THE SMELL CAN

WHAT IS YOUR LEAST FAVORITE SMELL?

Smelly socks?

Dad's aftershave?

Rotting vegetables?

The bottom
of your
school bag?

POO!

Rotten eggs?

Mom's perfume?

Horse manure?

WHAT ELSE CAN YOU THINK OF?

WHAT A LOAD OF TRASH!

TRASH FACT

During a year, an average family will probably throw away about 1.5 tons of trash

That's like throwing away HALF AN ELEPHANT every year!

TRASH FACT

Among the things thrown away each year in the United States are . . .

1.6 billion pens,
16 billion diapers,
220 million tires!
7 million automobiles are scrapped!

TRASH FACT

If you heaped up all the trash thrown away in the United States each year, it would cover 1,000 soccer fields with piles of waste 30 stories high.

SCRATCH FACT

Did you know that every time you scratch an itch, you let loose a very small cloud of dead skin and hair? This is what makes a lot of the dust in a house!

DO WE NEED TO THROW AWAY SO MANY THINGS?

Most of the trash in your trash can is empty containers and packaging. For example, every plastic bottle you throw away costs money to make.

When you buy the drink you have to pay for the bottle as well. When you throw the bottle away it's like putting money down a drain.

We spend millions of dollars getting rid of trash. Garbage trucks like this cost a fortune to build and use.

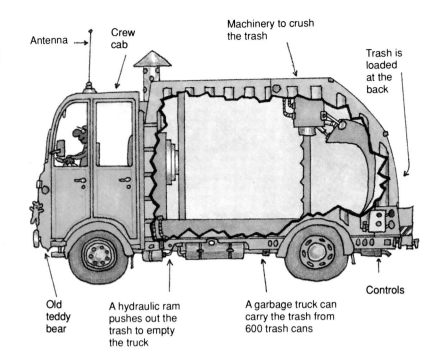

Antenna
Crew cab
Machinery to crush the trash
Trash is loaded at the back
Old teddy bear
A hydraulic ram pushes out the trash to empty the truck
A garbage truck can carry the trash from 600 trash cans
Controls

After the trash is collected it's often buried in huge holes in the ground. These holes are usually called garbage dumps. People who dig the holes for dumping trash call them landfill sites. They think this sounds better than "garbage dumps."

LANDFILL SITE

GARBAGE DUMP

BUT HERE ARE THREE REASONS WHY LANDFILL IS A BAD IDEA.

Reason 1: We are running out of places to dump trash!

The landfill site's full up... so we're delivering trash today!

Reason 2: Remember the smell of rotting trash?

METHANE GAS

Methane gas is not only smelly! It's also dangerous because it's poisonous and . . . E X P L O S I V E !

Reason 3: Animals that set up home on landfill sites can spread diseases. A garbage dump is a great place for mice, insects, and rats to live! In fact it's like one big holiday resort for them!

Trash is often burned to save space. If you look at a bonfire before it has been lit, it looks like this.

When it has been burned it makes a smaller pile, like this. The smaller pile is much easier to dispose of.

Some towns burn their household trash in a special factory.
These buildings have a large oven inside called an incinerator.
Using these incinerators helps to solve the rat problem!

Power stations use coal, oil, gas, or nuclear fuel to give us electricity and hot water.

An incinerator can do the same job much more cheaply by burning trash instead! This is called energy recovery.

Plus . . . the leftover ashes can be buried or used to make fertilizers to help plants grow better.

Sometimes trash is only half burned by mistake. When this happens, the incinerator can pour out smoke and deadly gases!

Some towns and cities dump their trash in the sea. Careless dumping of waste makes the ocean more polluted!

We must be more careful about what is thrown away. Waste chemicals and other trash dumped in the sea can easily poison fish for years afterward. And then . . .

WHO EATS THE FISH?

One way to use trash is called composting. In composting, trash is stored in containers until it rots away.

The material that is left is called compost, and it is full of nutrients that plants need. This works well for many kinds of trash.

In commercial composting, the compost is made in huge containers. Then it is mixed with chemicals to make fertilizers for farms and gardens.

Many gardeners make their own compost from yard clippings, potato peelings, and other vegetable matter. Then they add it to the soil in their gardens.

HOW TO MAKE A COMPOST HEAP
IN A TRASH CAN

1. Making compost is a messy job.
Get an old trash can and put it
in an unused part of your yard.
Ask an adult to make two rows of
drainage holes in it.

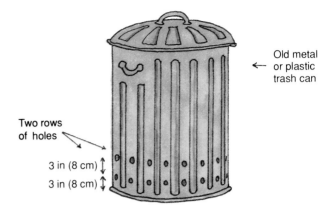

Old metal
← or plastic
trash can

Two rows
of holes

3 in (8 cm)

3 in (8 cm)

2. Then you need sand and small bits
of broken pottery, some pieces of wood,
some earthworms that you can find in
your garden soil, and some peat from a
garden center.

3. Put them in the can like this.

4. Add your chopped up waste vegetables.
Put the worms in the waste food. They eat
the vegetable matter and turn it into soil
that has a lot of nitrogen in it. Plants need
nitrogen to grow properly.

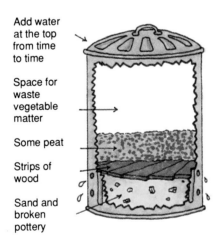

Add water
at the top
from time
to time

Space for
waste
vegetable
matter

Some peat

Strips of
wood

Sand and
broken
pottery

POINTS TO NOTE

Sort out the worms and put them back in
the can when you use the compost. You
can keep the same sand and wood for
each batch of compost.

It will take a few months to make useful
compost, but the worms live a long time,
so you can keep on using the compost
heap for ages!

BEYOND COMPOST

Composting is a good way to use some kinds of trash. But composting doesn't work for everything. Many types of plastic don't rot away, and metals have to be taken out of the trash before it is put in the compost heap, so that they don't poison the fertilizer.

This all takes a long time, and a lot of good trash is still wasted.

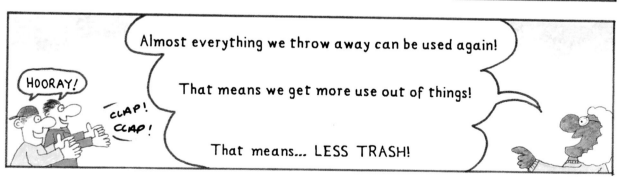

IT'S EVEN BETTER TO USE THINGS
OVER AND OVER AGAIN.
USING THINGS OVER AND OVER
AGAIN IS CALLED . . .

RECYCLING!

Almost everything you put in your trash can may be recycled. But . . . only a small amount of trash actually is recycled.

We could save millions of dollars every year by recycling the items that we just throw away. That's like throwing money away!

Also: we spend even more money on waste disposal!

Some charities make a lot of money from recycling. They will be pleased to take your old clothing, furniture, toys, and so on. Why not take that old unwanted shirt to a charity shop instead of throwing it away? The charity shop can sell it and use the money to help people.

COATS
SHOES
TOYS
SCARVES
HATS
GLOVES

There are lots of charities. Look for them in the phone book.

Choose your favorite charity and support it with . . .

RECYCLING!

GO FOR GOLD!

In the old days, prospectors traveled for miles to look for gold.
You only have to travel to your trash can to find your gold mine!
Here's what you need to be the well-dressed recycler.

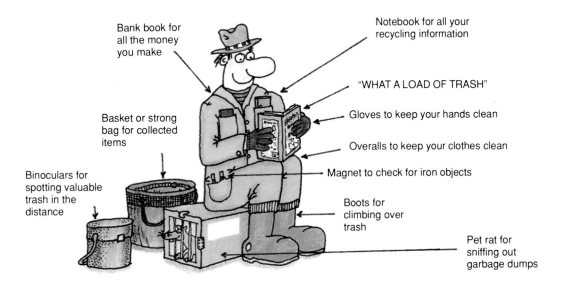

Bank book for all the money you make

Notebook for all your recycling information

Basket or strong bag for collected items

"WHAT A LOAD OF TRASH"

Gloves to keep your hands clean

Overalls to keep your clothes clean

Binoculars for spotting valuable trash in the distance

Magnet to check for iron objects

Boots for climbing over trash

Pet rat for sniffing out garbage dumps

HOW TO MAKE A RECYCLING NOTEBOOK

1. Get about 20 pieces of scrap paper. Unused pages in old notebooks are best. The insides of used envelopes will do.

2. Find a piece of stiff cardboard about twice as wide as the paper.

3. Get an old shoelace.

4. Put them all together like this . . .

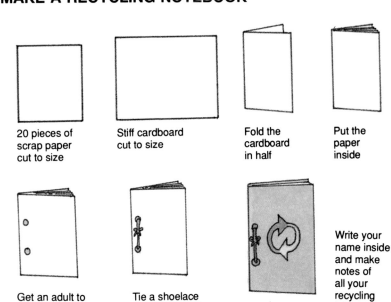

20 pieces of scrap paper cut to size

Stiff cardboard cut to size

Fold the cardboard in half

Put the paper inside

Get an adult to make two holes

Tie a shoelace through the holes

Write your name inside and make notes of all your recycling information

THE LIFE CYCLE OF A GLASS BOTTLE

START HERE

1. Take back all your returnable bottles. Save all your other glass bottles and jars.

2. Take off the lids. Keep them for recycling!

3. Wash out the bottles.

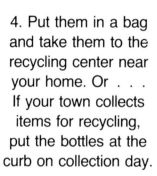

4. Put them in a bag and take them to the recycling center near your home. Or . . . If your town collects items for recycling, put the bottles at the curb on collection day.

5. A truck takes the bottles from the recycling center to a bottle warehouse, where they are stored until the glass factory is ready to take them.

12. You buy bottles and jars of your favorite foods and drinks. Soon they are empty and ready to go around again!

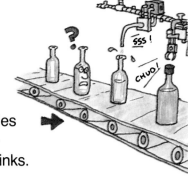

11. The finished bottles are sold to people who make food and drinks.

10. The new bottles are checked to see if they've been made properly. Badly made bottles go back to be melted down again.

9. The gobs are molded into the right shapes.

8. The melted glass is cut into chunks called gobs, which are the right size to be made into bottles.

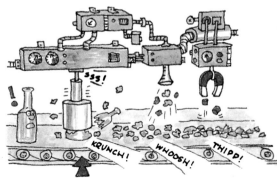

6. At the glass factory, the bottles are crushed. Magnets and cleaning machines take out any bits of metal and plastic.

7. The crushed glass (or cullet, as it's called) is heated until it melts.

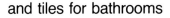
Factories can make all of these things out of old glass:

bricks for building houses

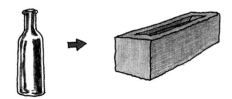

and tiles for bathrooms

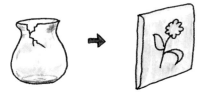

and sandpaper for smoothing wood

and fiberglass for furniture and boats.

You can use jars for lots of things.

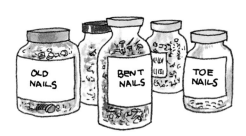

Keep your nuts and bolts in them.

Paint them and use them as flower vases.

Try to think of more uses for your bottles and jars.
Write down your ideas in your recycling notebook.
Every bottle you rescue from the trash can is valuable to us all!

BOTTLE RESCUE

One ton of old glass used saves 135 quarts of oil

SAVES ENERGY

It takes less fuel to make new glass from old bottles than from raw materials.

SAVES MONEY

Each bottle you recycle is one less for a trash collector to collect. It costs money to collect trash.

SAVES RESOURCES

Using old glass to make new glass means we use less of our raw materials.

PROTECTS THE ENVIRONMENT

Less digging or quarrying for raw materials.

WHAT TO DO

1. Always try to buy your drinks in returnable bottles.

2. Take your other bottles and jars to a recycling center.

TRY THIS TONGUE-TWISTER

BOTTLES
BROUGHT BACK

BEAT BROKEN
BOTTLES BY FAR.

Erk!

TO THE DOCTOR

Most bottles and jars are used just once and are then thrown away!
Some bottles are recycled. You pay a deposit on some bottles.
Very often, careless people throw these away. If you collected them
and returned them, you would make money and help to save glass!

WHAT TO DO

1. Always buy returnable bottles if you can.

2. Check up on your local shops to find out which types of bottles they will take back.

3. Write down what you find out in your recycling notebook.

4. Collect all your empty bottles and ask your neighbors if they have any. Take any returnable bottles back to the right shops and take the others to the recycling center.

Broken glass can be used for all sorts of surprising things. In America
and in some parts of Europe, glass is used to make roads. It is crushed
into tiny pieces and is used like gravel. This is called glassphalt.
It reflects headlight beams, making the road easier to see at night.

THE PAPER MOUNTAIN

The abominable paperman!

A lot of the stuff we throw away is made of paper and cardboard. Most of this cardboard is used packaging, like your corn-flakes box and your milk carton. In the United States, almost 60,000,000 tons of paper and cardboard are used each year. Most of this paper and cardboard is made from the wood of trees. Very little of it is recycled—most of it is just thrown away after it is used. So every year, more trees are cut down. About 220,000,000 trees are cut down every year just to make U.S. newspapers! But we need trees for more than paper and cardboard. Take a look:

DO YOU LIKE READING
HORROR STORIES?

You do? Well, read on.

The following facts are deadlier than Dracula, more frightening than Frankenstein, and even more worrying than the Wolfman! Because they are true, and happening RIGHT NOW!

RECYCLING BASKET

FACT ONE

One square mile (2.5 square kilometers) of Earth's forests is destroyed every five minutes to make room for food crops or to get wood to make paper.

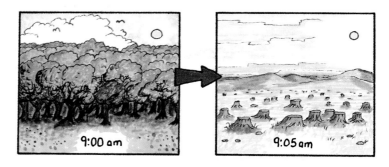

9:00 am

9:05 am

FACT TWO

Many animals can live only in forests. When we cut down trees, we take away their homes, so many of them DIE!

FACT THREE

Trees give off oxygen, so forests are important for keeping up the supply of air that we breathe!

SNIFF!

Even the plants that you have in your house produce life-giving oxygen.

FACT FOUR

For every 1,000 trees we cut down, we only plant 25 in their place.

If we carry on this way, soon there won't be any trees left at all!

But it's still not too late!

WHAT YOU CAN DO

1. Save all your cardboard and waste paper.

SAVE PAPER TO SAVE TREES AND WILDLIFE!

2. Try to get your teacher or club leader to start a collection of paper and cardboard.

3. Make sure you keep your paper dry and store it well away from fires.

4. When you have run out of space to store the paper, ask an adult to take it to the recycling center. A paper merchant will take the paper from the center to a factory, which will use it to make more paper.

MAKING THE MOST OF METALS

Sooner or later, we will use up all the Earth's metals unless we try to save them.

Metals could run out in about 100 years if we use them up as quickly as we are doing now.

Luckily, metals are very easy to recycle! Here are some of the more common metals you may find.

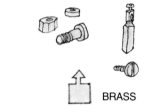

ALUMINUM

BRASS

COPPER

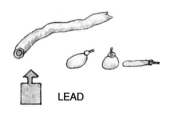

LEAD

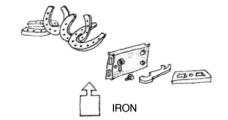

IRON

STEEL

WHAT TO DO

Learn to identify these common metals. Make notes of their uses in your notebook.

You can sell all your old scrap metal to scrap metal dealers. Find out if there's one near your home.

Write the names and addresses of the metal dealers in your notebook.

When you've collected a few pounds of metal, get an adult to take you to the closest scrap metal dealer to sell it.

METAL DEALERS

Scrap metal dealers sell the metal they collect to metal working factories. They often crush it into large blocks first, to make it easier to transport. Sometimes, you can tell what a block was made from by examining it. Why don't you try this quiz?

Here are some blocks made of compacted scrap metal. What were they? Match each name on the right to a block on the left.

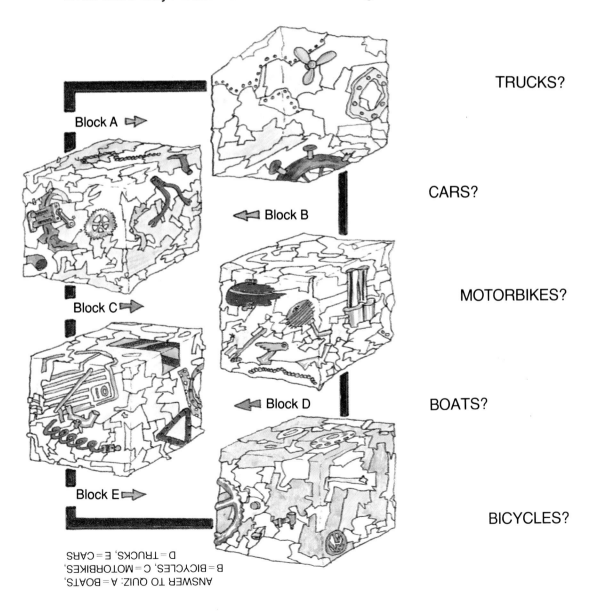

Block A

Block B

Block C

Block D

Block E

TRUCKS?

CARS?

MOTORBIKES?

BOATS?

BICYCLES?

ANSWER TO QUIZ: A = BOATS, B = BICYCLES, C = MOTORBIKES, D = TRUCKS, E = CARS

MORE METAL FACTS

Did you know that there is almost no tin in a tin can? Tin is far too expensive to be used for making cans that are thrown away!
It takes up to 31 barrels of oil to make 1 ton of aluminum.

But when scrap aluminum is recycled, it takes only 2 barrels of oil. Today most drink cans are made out of valuable aluminum. Some are made from steel.

In America, 110 billion food and drink cans are bought each year! What did you do with the last empty can you had?

PENALTY!

WHAT TO DO

Use a magnet to check which metal the cans are made of.

The magnet will stick to steel cans but not to aluminum ones.

STEEL CANS

ALUMINUM CANS

You pay a deposit on many drink cans, just as you do on bottles. Return these cans to the store.

Save the other cans to take to the recycling center.

FROM RAGS TO RICHES!

Try not to think of old clothes as being just useless rags.
Remember . . . trash is only trash if you THINK it is!

RAG FACT

Did you know that old rags are used in making of bank notes? That really is rags to riches!

Charity shops will be very pleased to have your clean old clothes.

You can take your old clothes to rummage sales. Look in the newspaper to find out where and when they take place. Write the information in your notebook.

RAG FACT

Some cloth makers buy old clothes and shred them to make material for new clothes. Part of the sweater you're wearing right now might be made of the old socks you threw out last year!

When you grow out of old clothes, you could pass them on to friends or to the younger members of your family.

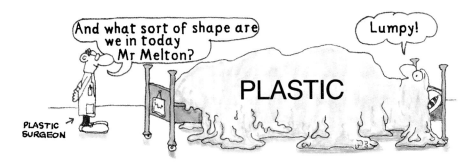

PLASTIC

Plastic is cheap and easy to use. Just about anything can be made from plastic these days.

Plastic is a great invention.

But . . . it gives us a lot of problems!

Most plastic is made from oil. We are using up our supplies of oil at a frightening speed.

When plastic is being made, both poisonous wastes and gases can escape into the environment.

It's also not easy to recycle plastic. So it gets buried or burned. That means more pollution.

The easiest plastic to identify is called PET.
No, it's not a dog or a cat or a fish! It's short for

POLYETHYLENETEREPHTHALATE

This is almost as hard to say as

FLOCCIPAUCINIHILIPILIFICATION

which is the longest word in the Oxford English Dictionary.

PET is used to make returnable bottles for soda and other drinks. You pay deposit on these bottles, and you can take them back to the store. The bottles are taken to a factory, where they are shredded into tiny bits. Shredded PET is used to make carpet fiber and fiberfill for sleeping bags and other items.

Some other kinds of plastic can be recycled, too. Plastic foam from fast-food containers can be melted and made into plastic trash cans and food trays. Plastic milk jugs can be melted and mixed with other kinds of plastic to make new bottles for detergent and other non-food items.

When you can't recycle plastic containers, try to think of ways to use them instead of throwing them away.

HOW TO GROW A PET PLANT

You can use empty PET bottles to grow plants in.

1. Cut a bottle in half and make a few holes in each half.

2. Put soil and compost from your heap (page 18) in the bottom half.

3. Put it on an old saucer. Make holes in the soil and put your seeds in.

4. After a few weeks the plant begins to grow.

5. Stick the top half back on to protect the plant.

6. Keep the soil damp by watering through the top.

WHAT'S LEFT

Most waste can be recycled, but you can't recycle all of it by yourself.

OIL

A lot of waste oil is poured into drains, causing pollution. Some garages collect old oil that can be cleaned and used again. Many towns have collection programs for oil and other such dangerous waste products.

SAWDUST

Sawdust can be recycled to make chip-board for furniture. It can also be used for cat litter and to keep your rabbit warm in winter!

WASTE FOOD

You can use some waste food on your compost heap. In some places, pig farmers buy leftover food from school dinners to feed their pigs!

EXPERT'S EXAM

By now you should be an expert recycler! Here's a quiz to test your knowledge.

How many of these things could be recycled?

GLASSES

ASHES FROM FIRES

OLD BOOT

BENT NAILS AND SCREWS

OLD UMBRELLA

OLD BOOK

WORN-OUT CAR BATTERY

A BONE

OLD TIRE

BROKEN TOY

OLD TV

OLD FRONT DOOR

OLD SOCK

USED BATHWATER

OLD SUIT

WORN-OUT RECORD

USED GARBAGE TRUCK

ANSWER TO EXPERT'S EXAM: EVERYTHING!

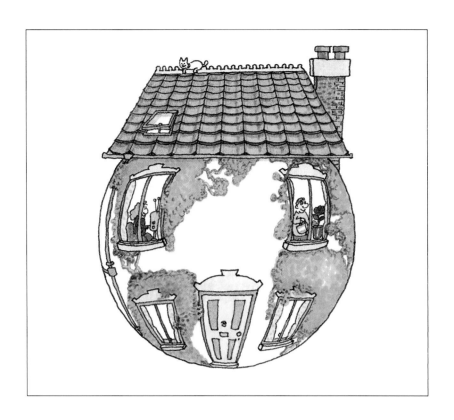

IT'S UP TO ALL OF US TO TAKE CARE OF THE EARTH.
IT'S OUR HOME.

Recycling can help save our supplies and
keep our world safer and healthier!

Recycling means keeping your trash can
as empty as possible!

Remember to

Recycle as much as you can.
Tell your friends about recycling.
Get other people to collect paper, bottles, and cans.
Think before you throw anything away!

Every little bit helps. Now . . .

HOW ARE YOU GOING TO RECYCLE THIS BOOK?

FIND OUT MORE

Now that you've learned how to rescue your household waste, find out more about trash and recycling. Visit a recycling center near your home to see how trash is collected and separated.

Here are some books to look for in the library:

50 Simple Things Kids Can Do to Save the Earth, by

the Earth Works Group (Andrews and McMeel, 1990)

Garbage: Our Endangered Planet, by Karen O'Connor

(Lucent Books, 1989)

Too Much Garbage, by Patricia Lauber (Garrard, 1974)

INDEX